DENNY AB
AND TH
FARMLAND M USEUM

CAMBRIDGESHIRE

Richard Wood MA (Cantab), BEd

Denny Abbey was established in 1159 as an offshoot, or dependent 'cell', of Ely Cathedral Priory. Over the following 400 years – and uniquely among religious houses in England – the abbey was occupied successively by Benedictine monks, the lay order known as Knights Templar, and an order of Franciscan nuns, the Poor Clares. Each community left its distinctive mark, and adapted the buildings to its particular needs. When the Countess of Pembroke brought the Poor Clares to Denny in the 14th century, she converted part of the existing church into a house for herself, unwittingly securing the building's long-term survival.

With the closure of the abbey by order of Henry VIII in 1539, Denny became a farm. The former monastic buildings were adapted once again to provide a farmhouse and barns, which they remained until the 1960s. The Farmland Museum, adjacent to the abbey remains, was set up in 1997. Its displays represent aspects of Cambridgeshire farming and rural life, complementing the earlier monastic history and bringing the story of Denny up to date.

ACKNOWLEDGEMENTS

The author would like to acknowledge the detailed research and contribution to scholarship in J. G. Coad's guidebook to Denny Abbey, first published in 1984. The author and publisher would also like to thank the staff and trustees of the Farmland Museum, especially Kate Brown and Corrina Bower, for their generous assistance and advice during the production of this guidebook.

FURTHER READING

P. M. Christie and J. G. Coad, 'Excavations at Denny Abbey', *Archaeological Journal*, 137 (1980), pp. 138–279

J. G. Coad, *Denny Abbey*, English Heritage: London, 1984

A. Day, *Farming in the Fens: A Portrait in Old Photographs and Prints*, SB Publications: Seaford, East Sussex, 1995

J. Poster and D. Sherlock, 'Denny Abbey: The Nuns' Refectory', *Proceedings of the Cambridge Antiquarian Society*, 76 (1987), pp. 67–82

Denny Abbey and the Farmland Museum
Ely Road, Waterbeach, Cambridge, CB25 9PQ
Tel: 01223 860988/860489

English Heritage
1 Waterhouse Square, 138–142 Holborn,
London EC1N 2ST
© English Heritage 2003
Published by English Heritage 2003
Revised reprint 2012, 2016
All photographs are copyright of English Heritage, unless otherwise stated. Revised reprint photography by Pat Payne.

Edited by Sarah Yates
Designed by Pauline Hull
Picture research by Diana Phillips
Plan by Richard Morris
Printed in England by Park Communications Ltd
C16, 06/16, 04161, ISBN 978 1 85074 849 6

www.english-heritage.org.uk
www.dennyfarmlandmuseum.org.uk

FSC
www.fsc.org
MIX
Paper from responsible sources
FSC® C001785

❖ CONTENTS ❖

TOUR

HISTORY

TOUR

❖

THE ABBEY:
SOUTH SIDE

The tour begins on the south side of the buildings, near the second-hand bookshop. The ground plan (on the inside back cover) may help to guide you around the abbey remains.

What was Denny Abbey? The south side of the building looks like a handsome farmhouse – and that is exactly what it was from the 1540s to the 1960s. The large, rectangular sash windows were inserted some time in the early 19th century to replace earlier, probably arched, windows. This side of the house received the most sunlight, and photographs from the mid-20th century show an attractive garden here.

But, look closer, and you will notice several unusual features. Though the walls are built partly of brick, there is also a surprisingly large amount of stonework. Good building stone is difficult to obtain in Cambridgeshire, and was used only for important buildings such as castles, churches and monasteries. Traces of blocked-up windows and doorways suggest that the appearance of the building has changed several

times. The farmhouse was, in fact, adapted from the much older structure of the abbey church that existed here from 1159 to 1539. Unusually, there are no traces of other monastic buildings on this side of the abbey. At Denny, the normal practice of building the living quarters – kitchen, refectory, dormitory and offices – to the south of the church was reversed: the remains of these lie to the north.

Key to south side of abbey:
1 *Blocked door to a garderobe (privy), 13th century; archaeologists found evidence of a cesspit below.*
2 *Brickwork and Georgian-style sash windows, probably early 19th century.*
3 *Blocked farmhouse doorway built on remains of doorway from late 14th century.*
4 *Remains of garderobe window with cesspit below, 14th century.*
5 *Narrow slit windows lighting a spiral staircase inside, 14th century.*
6 *Stone wall of south transept (arm) of church, 1170s.*
7 *Tudor brick chimney, 1540s.*

Denny through History

❖

The buildings you now see at Denny are somewhat like a jumbled architectural jigsaw puzzle. Before you discover how the pieces fit together, it may help to know a little of their history. These two pages provide a brief summary of the story of the abbey, farm and museum. Some parts (such as the nuns' church) have been destroyed, while others (such as the south side of the abbey) were modified in several different periods. The bird's eye view drawing on pages 16–17 will help you to identify each part.

BEFORE THE ABBEY

This site was inhabited in Roman times, almost 2,000 years ago. Some fragments of Roman pottery were found during excavations at Denny, and a raised earth trackway of this date lies in the fields to the east of the abbey. It is not known whether the site was occupied between the late 4th and the mid-12th centuries.

Roman coins were unearthed during excavations at Denny Abbey

1159–70 THE BENEDICTINE CHURCH

The first monks at Denny were Benedictines from Ely who started building a church here by 1159. Though its east end was later knocked down, the transepts (the north–south section) survive, and the nave (the western part) was also begun at this time. You can identify the Benedictine church by the remains of its thick walls and its heavy round arches supported by pillars with capitals (the top part) decorated with a wavy scallop pattern. Later, many of the open arches were filled in, and new walls and floors inserted.

Two Benedictine monks, from a medieval manuscript

1170–1308 THE KNIGHTS TEMPLAR

The Knights Templar (see page 8) took over Denny after 1170 for use as a sort of retirement home or hospital for elderly members of the order. They probably finished building the church, which was quite small and in the shape of a cross with arms of equal length. The round-arched door at the west end and the capitals with pointed leaf decoration date from the Templar period. Many of the earthworks in the surrounding fields – remnants of ponds, water channels and other moated enclosures – also belong to this period.

A Templar Knight, wearing a cloak marked with a cross

1327–1538
THE POOR CLARES

1539
SUPPRESSION OF THE MONASTERIES

1544–1947
THE FARM

AFTER 1947:
FROM FARM TO MUSEUM

Some years after the Templars were forced to leave Denny, the buildings were acquired by Mary de Valence, Countess of Pembroke. She set up an abbey here for an order of nuns known as the Poor Clares. The countess converted most of the existing church into a private house for herself, later used by the abbess, with a new guest hall replacing the south aisle. The east end of the church was knocked down, and a new, larger church built in its place. This was also later destroyed, but modern concrete lines in the grass on the east side show where it stood. The surviving refectory and various other buildings, now ruined, also date from the nuns' time.

Saint Clare, founder of the order of Poor Clares

In the 1530s, following the break with papal authority, Henry VIII ordered the closure of all monasteries in England, and sold off their lands and contents. In 1539 a property speculator, Edward Elrington, bought Denny Abbey. He started dismantling some of the buildings for their valuable stone. The nuns' church and some of the domestic

THE NATIONAL ARCHIVES

THE ART ARCHIVE

Henry VIII, who ordered the closure of the English monasteries

buildings on the north side were taken down at this time. In 1544 Denny reverted to the king when Elrington exchanged it for other lands.

The Countess of Pembroke had already converted most of the original abbey church into a house. With a few modifications, the Tudor

The nuns' refectory, in an illustration of 1828, when it was used as a barn

owners found that it made a convenient farmhouse. The gable-ended wall on the south side of the abbey was rebuilt, mainly in brick, to accommodate a large chimney for a kitchen. Other later changes account for the different walls and floors you see today, as well as the farmhouse-style windows and doors. The former nuns' refectory also survived as a barn, and a second barn was built in the 17th century.

In 1947 Denny Abbey came into the care of the Ministry of Works. In the late 1960s, with the last farm tenant gone, archaeologists began to uncover the evidence of the building's earlier use. To reveal more of the monastic structures, some later additions were removed. The result is the curious, but fascinating jumble of building styles and phases seen today. Since 1997 the Farmland Museum has completed the story of the site with displays about Cambridgeshire farming and country life, so familiar to the later occupants of Denny.

The stone barn of the Farmland Museum

The abbey from the west, showing the round-arched doorway of the Templar church (left) and the part of the building that was once the priest's house (right)

Go round to the west side of the building.

EARTHWORKS

Look across the fields to see remains of earthworks associated with the Templars and the medieval causeway that was once the main entrance to the abbey from Waterbeach. Near the present road are the medieval fishponds, which kept the religious communities supplied with fish for the table.

WEST END

The original church door, now blocked, is recognisable by its heavy round arch with chevron decoration. This was carved from clunch, a soft stone, unfortunately now badly worn. The style of the door dates from soon after 1170, when the Templars took over Denny. The Benedictine monks

Several blocked entrances on the north-west side show how the abbey was progressively adapted for different uses

had planned a longer church nave with four bays (sections), which would have extended it to where the low wall now stands. But the Templars needed only a small chapel where they could attend Mass, so they completed the church with only two bays to the nave. Notice the site of a burial near the door. The skeleton found here had been buried with a pewter chalice and an unusual round lead disc marked with a geometric cross. It was probably that of a 13th-century priest who served the Templars. The present entrance door and windows were inserted in the early 19th century, when the building was a farmhouse. This part, however, was once a separate structure, built in the 13th century probably to house the Templars' priest. It was the Countess of Pembroke who, a century later, incorporated this small building into the large new guest hall on the south side of the church.

NORTH SIDE

Go round to the left of the church to take a closer look at the buildings from the north.

The level grassy rectangle here was the monastic garden, and the remains of a medieval well can still be seen. Some of the domestic buildings of the Templars, and later the nuns, stood around here, but were demolished in the 1540s. The nuns' dormitory, however, survived for a further 200 years. This two-storey building once extended north from the north transept. The gabled end wall has a large opening (with modern glazing), and traces of two smaller blocked doorways. These all, at different periods, gave direct access to the church from the first-floor dormitory. This arrangement was required by the nuns' daily pattern of prayer, beginning at 2 a.m. with the service of Nocturns, after which they returned to bed.

❖ BUILDING THE ABBEY ❖

Monasteries were not constructed by the monks themselves, but by skilled professional builders – masons, carpenters, leadworkers, glaziers and others – under the direction of a master mason. The stone used at Denny was expensive to buy and transport from the quarries. For edges, smooth facing stones, and window and door surrounds the masons employed hard dressed stone from Barnack in Northamptonshire. Elsewhere, they used rough Kentish ragstone, ironstone from Norfolk and soft white clunch from south Cambridgeshire. The thickness of pillars and walls can be deceptive: often they consist of rubble and mortar with only the outer layer made of solid stone blocks.

THE ART ARCHIVE

A manuscript of 1475, showing medieval builders and a mason's lodge

On site, the builders dug foundations. As the walls grew higher, they set up wooden scaffolding and used pulleys or wheels to haul up baskets of small stones or larger blocks of cut stone. Arches were constructed around wooden templates until, with the final keystone in place, the support could be removed. The master mason worked in a temporary building on site, called the lodge. For precise work, such as mouldings of arches, or window tracery, he produced wooden patterns against which the stones could be cut. Inside Denny, where the stone is less worn, are marks made by chisels and saws. There are also some masons' marks, which were used as a guide to show the required position for each stone.

THE KNIGHTS
❖ TEMPLAR ❖

The Templars were an order of 'soldier monks' founded in 1118 to defend the Kingdom of Jerusalem against attack, ensuring that pilgrims would always be able to visit the holy places associated with the life of Christ. As soldiers, they had a reputation for great ferocity and bravery, but, like monks, they also took vows of poverty, chastity and obedience. In the 1120s Bernard of Clairvaux, the French monastic reformer, compiled a 'rule', or set of instructions, for them, and in 1128 the pope confirmed this and granted them privileges, for example freedom from the authority of bishops. The same year, the Templars arrived in England, and established their headquarters at Temple Church, London. New recruits and donations of land and money began to pour in, and for more than a century the Templars were a powerful force in the Church and kingdoms of Europe. However, by the late 13th century the tide had turned against them. Bishops and rulers resented their wealth and secrecy, and, when Jerusalem was captured by the Turks in 1291, the Templars lost their main purpose. Following the lead of other European rulers, in 1308 Edward II ordered the arrest of all Templars in England, and in 1312 the order was disbanded by the pope.

THE ART ARCHIVE

A Templar knight on crusade, from a 12th-century wall painting

GROUND FLOOR

Retrace your steps, enter the building through the former farmhouse door and stop on the raised walkway inside.

The floor plan (right) may help you to identify the main features inside the building. Clearly, what you see today was never intended to look like this. Various parts of the building have been removed to reveal some of the earlier features that were hidden under later modifications.

Evidence of each of the main phases – Benedictine, Templar, Poor Clare and farmhouse – can be seen. Some features, such as the sturdy stone pillars, correspond to the building's original use as a church. Others, including various internal walls, windows and doorways, are associated with its gradual conversion to domestic use. As the remains of the bread oven show, the once grand crossing at the centre of the church ended up serving as a farmhouse bakery.

The ground-floor crossing; the south transept, fireplace and kitchen are to the left

PLAN OF THE ABBEY

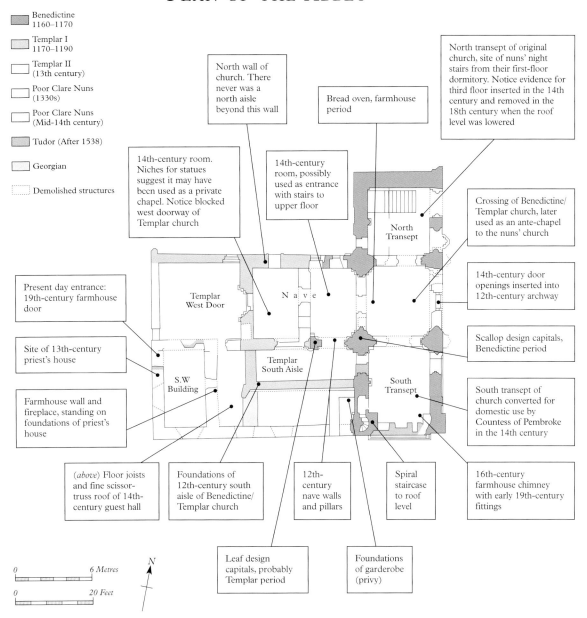

Benedictine
1160–1170

Templar I
1170–1190

Templar II
(13th century)

Poor Clare Nuns
(1330s)

Poor Clare Nuns
(Mid-14th century)

Tudor (After 1538)

Georgian

Demolished structures

North wall of church. There never was a north aisle beyond this wall

Bread oven, farmhouse period

North transept of original church, site of nuns' night stairs from their first-floor dormitory. Notice evidence for third floor inserted in the 14th century and removed in the 18th century when the roof level was lowered

14th-century room. Niches for statues suggest it may have been used as a private chapel. Notice blocked west doorway of Templar church

14th-century room, possibly used as entrance with stairs to upper floor

Crossing of Benedictine/ Templar church, later used as an ante-chapel to the nuns' church

Present day entrance: 19th-century farmhouse door

Templar West Door

N a v e

North Transept

14th-century door openings inserted into 12th-century archway

Site of 13th-century priest's house

Scallop design capitals, Benedictine period

Templar South Aisle

S.W Building

South Transept

Farmhouse wall and fireplace, standing on foundations of priest's house

South transept of church converted for domestic use by Countess of Pembroke in the 14th century

(above) Floor joists and fine scissor-truss roof of 14th-century guest hall

Foundations of 12th-century south aisle of Benedictine/ Templar church

12th-century nave walls and pillars

Spiral staircase to roof level

16th-century farmhouse chimney with early 19th-century fittings

Leaf design capitals, probably Templar period

Foundations of garderobe (privy)

0   6 Metres

0   20 Feet

N

View from the Countess of Pembroke's first-floor chamber, looking north. New walls and doorways were later inserted in the original arches of the crossing at first-floor level

Traces of paintwork in the first-floor west rooms

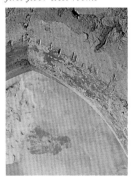

Upper Floor
North Transept

In the north transept, go up the modern wooden stairs and stop on the landing.

The landing provides a good vantage point from which the scale and layout of the original church can be appreciated. The first-floor level, and another one above, were inserted in the 1340s, when the church was converted into private apartments for the Countess of Pembroke. She was a regular visitor and died here in 1377, after which date the abbess probably lived in these quarters. The wide round arches of the church were partly filled in, incorporating smaller arched doors suitable for domestic use. In this transept there must have been a balcony and stairs connecting the countess's rooms to the new church (entered from below) and

perhaps to the nuns' dormitory (beyond the north wall, opposite).

Crossing

Go through the arched doorway.

This square room was formed out of the central crossing of the original church. The stonework of the Norman pillars and arches, so long hidden behind later masonry, has been revealed. This is high-quality limestone from Barnack, Northamptonshire. The stone would have been roughly cut to shape at the quarry, according to designs sent by the Denny mason, then finished on site. The chisel and saw marks are clearly visible. The capitals are carved with the scallop design associated with the first, Benedictine, stage of building. Below the later window in the east wall is an old stone sill. This is all that remains of a window through which the countess could watch Mass being celebrated at the far end of the new church. As she was not a member of the order, she did not worship with the nuns.

West Rooms

Go through the doorway that is on your right as you enter the crossing.

The rooms to the west of the crossing were formed from the two bays of the original nave. In the first room a small arched doorway in the north wall led to the nuns' guest hall, while other doors once opened on to the private apartments. These details suggest that the first room once housed a staircase from an entrance below. In the second room notice the blocked west window of the Templars' church – the fireplace was added much later when this building was a farmhouse. The remains of the original upper (clerestory) windows, which lit the nave of the church, are also visible. The capitals at the west end with the pointed leaf design may indicate the point at which the Templars took over the building of the church from the Benedictines. Some original – or, at least, early – red paintwork survives around the 14th-century door arch, indicating that these rooms would once have been colourfully painted.

South Room

Return to the crossing and go into the room on your right.

This room, formed in the south transept of the church, was probably the countess's private chamber – her best bed-sitting room. It would have been less spacious than it appears today, with a low ceiling allowing space for a second floor above. As if to emphasise the private nature of this room, the spiral staircase in the corner bypasses it, going directly from ground-floor to second-floor level. The room was no doubt warm and well-lit. There are remains of a fireplace in the west wall (to the right of the two arched openings), and

there was perhaps a large window in the south-facing wall, now replaced by the brick- and stonework of the Tudor farmhouse chimney stack.

The small arched door opening in the south-west corner led into a garderobe or privy – a seat with a single hole, perched above a pit below. When the pit was excavated, among other remains were found fig and grape seeds, suggesting that the original occupant enjoyed a more varied diet than the plain fare of the nuns. The wider arch to the right appears originally to have been a recessed cupboard – possibly housing, among other items, a small library of devotional books. It was later knocked through to form a doorway into the guest hall, and today it provides a good view into the remains of the hall. The timbers of the 14th-century roof survive as a fine example of scissor-truss construction.

The site of the nuns' first-floor guest hall, built above the original south aisle

Interior of the south transept, showing a Tudor fireplace inserted at second-floor level

NUNS' CHURCH

Retrace your steps and go down the stairs. Leave through the doorway to your left and turn to look at the east side of the building.

The east wall of the present building was once the west end of the Poor Clares' church, later demolished

You are now standing on the site of the 14th-century nuns' church, built by the Countess of Pembroke to replace the earlier Benedictine and Templar church. Almost nothing of the nuns' church remains, however, apart from the tall stone pillar to the right of the central arch. The matching pillar on the other side was removed in the 18th century and made into two gateposts, which still stand at the end of the drive off the A10 road. The remaining pillar gives an idea of the height of the nuns' church, especially as the present roof level is known to be much lower than that of the original. The nuns' church was significantly larger than its predecessor, but with the simple rectangular shape of an aisled chapel. The stone wall by the cottage indicates the position of the east end, and the lines of the north and south walls are marked out on the ground. Within these, the site of the east end of the original Benedictine church is also marked.

East Side

Like so much of Denny Abbey, the east wall displays an extraordinary medley of evidence of different architectural periods, styles and functions. The central blocked-up archway survives from the Benedictine church. The smaller archways show that the chancel (the eastern arm of the church containing the main altar) had aisles. Only a trace of the south aisle arch remains today, while the north aisle arch is partly obscured by the tall pillar of the nuns' church, described above. The pointed archway further to the right also belongs to the 14th-century rebuilding. It would have given access to the north aisle of the nuns' church from the night stairs via the old north transept. The present windows and doorways all date from the farmhouse period, but you can still see above the central door the sill of the small window through which the countess could observe services in her new church.

THE POOR CLARES ❖

For the second half of its history as a religious house, Denny housed an order of nuns known as Franciscans, Minoresses or Poor Clares. In 1212 St Clare 'renounced the world' and withdrew to the church of San Damiano at Assisi in northern Italy. She was soon joined by other women, following a rule of poverty prescribed

The dolegate of Abbess Elizabeth Throckmorton, which can still be seen at Coughton Court, Warwickshire

by Clare's friend St Francis. Over the next few years, other convents were formed, and in 1219 the Rule of St Clare – a sort of constitution for the order – was formally approved by the pope. The number of convents grew, though only three were founded in England, each through the influence of a wealthy patroness, such as the Countess of Pembroke at Denny. Today the order has over 20,000 nuns in 76 countries.

The nuns' way of life was in many ways similar to that of the original Benedictine monks at Denny. Their daily timetable consisted of periods of worship and prayer for the world, considered to be their main purpose. But as an enclosed order, they had minimal contact with the outside world. They were not allowed to possess property, and spoke rather than sang their services. They dressed simply in loose-fitting grey garments, spent much of the day in silence, fasted in the daytime throughout the

year (except on Christmas Day) and never ate meat. It was a rigorous way of life, but one that was maintained at Denny to the end.

The last abbess of Denny was Dame Elizabeth Throckmorton. When finally forced to abandon Denny in 1539, she retired to her family home at Coughton Court, Warwickshire. She took with her two or three nuns and also the dole gate from Denny. There it survives as a reminder of how the nuns' only communication with the outside world was via a narrow hatch, through which alms were doled out to the needy.

Nuns seated in choir stalls, from a medieval manuscript

The thatched refectory building, engraved by the Buck brothers in 1730, when it had been converted into a barn. The pulpit extension, and the former nuns' dormitory range in the background, were still standing at this date

REFECTORY

Go through the opening in the wall and across the grass to the former nuns' refectory.

Though this is now a detached building, it was once connected to the other parts of the abbey via a cloister – where the nuns could sit to read or meditate – and various covered passageways. The cloister lay between the church and the refectory, but its precise dimensions are not known as this part of the site has never been excavated.

If the refectory now looks more like a barn than a monastic building, that is because it was used as such for 400 years after the dissolution of the abbey. The entrance is through a pair of large doors in the south wall. There was once a matching opening in the opposite wall, though this has now been filled in with brickwork. Opening both sets of doors allowed a through draught – necessary when threshing grain – and also allowed access for large farm carts. It is possible, however, to imagine the building being used for its original purpose, as the nuns' dining hall, thanks to the survival of so much of the medieval structure.

The modern painting opposite the entrance shows how the refectory might have looked, based on evidence found in the building. It was a light room, with six windows on the north side and one large window on the east side, all now blocked, and one or more windows in the south wall. The kitchens were perhaps beyond the west end or east end wall, possibly in a detached structure as a precaution against fire. A raised pulpit was in a small extension on the north side: the nuns ate in silence listening to readings from the scriptures or other religious books. It was reached by steps, and its arched doorway and supports are still visible. A print of 1828 (see page 5) shows the extension still standing.

The refectory in 1951, in use as a barn

© CROWN COPYRIGHT NATIONAL MONUMENTS RECORD

MEDIEVAL FOOD
❖ AND FARMING ❖

Like most religious houses, Denny Abbey was largely self-sufficient in food. From its foundation the abbey owned lands in the surrounding countryside as well as in areas further afield, such as Yorkshire. While the estates further away paid their rents in cash, the nearer ones grew food directly for the abbey kitchens. The nuns' requirements were, in any case, quite limited – wheat or rye flour for baking bread, barley and some 'green stuff' (peas, cabbages, garlic, onions and leeks) for pottage (a thick soup), and milk for butter and cheese. Herbs, possibly grown within the abbey grounds, were used for flavouring food, and making medicines and ointments. Fish came from the abbey fish ponds, and fruit, usually eaten cooked rather than fresh, from nearby orchards.

The Denny home estate centred on the farm at Causeway End, Chittering, linked directly to the abbey by a raised trackway. Drier farmland, suitable for pasture or growing crops, was probably divided into narrow strips. Peasant farmers on the estate would have tended one or more strips, handing over a portion of their produce to the abbey bailiff and keeping the rest to sell or to feed their own families. Animals were kept, not only for milk and meat, but also for their dung, used to fertilise the land. Tilling the land was done either with hand tools or ploughs pulled by oxen. The closure of Denny as a religious house probably had little immediate impact on farming methods – improvements in livestock breeding, amalgamation of strips into larger hedged fields, and introduction of root crops and labour-saving machinery did not gather momentum until the late 18th or early 19th century.

Perhaps the most remarkable survival is that of much of the original 14th-century tiled floor. The plain tiles, with a dark green or black and yellow glaze, probably came from the tileworks at Bawsey, near King's Lynn, Norfolk. They are laid diagonally between three parallel rows of single tiles, but stop short of the walls. Around the walls are supports for a timber floor on which the nuns' tables and benches were set. The east end was raised to create a dais for the abbess and distinguished guests, who entered through a small private door at the east end of the south wall. Evidence of wood panelling around the lower part of the walls, with some painted decoration above, indicates that this room may have been less austere than it now seems. There was never a fireplace, so dining here must often have been a chilly experience.

Reconstruction painting by Terry Ball showing how the refectory might have looked in the 14th century

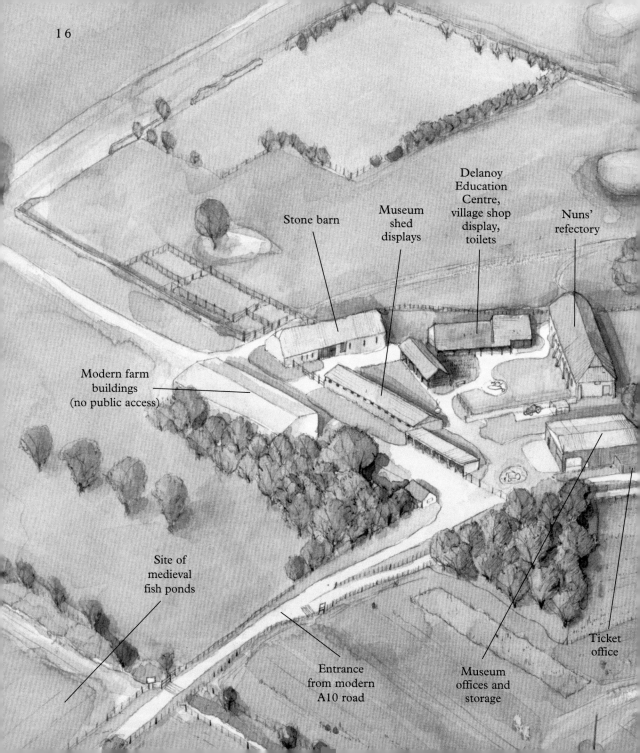

Stone barn

Museum shed displays

Delanoy Education Centre, village shop display, toilets

Nuns' refectory

Modern farm buildings (no public access)

Site of medieval fish ponds

Entrance from modern A10 road

Museum offices and storage

Ticket office

Farm walls, built of
re-used abbey stones

Walnut Tree
Cottage

Site of nuns'
church

Former abbey
buildings

Second-hand bookshop

Site of
medieval
causeway

Earthworks

Car park

Site of
abbey garden

*Bird's eye view of Denny Abbey and
the Farmland Museum by Judith Dobie*

Walnut Tree Cottage, a basic 'two up, two down' tied cottage for farmworkers and their families

The living room, with its typical 1940s and 1950s furnishings

WALNUT TREE COTTAGE

Go back across the grass to the cottage, opposite the east end of the main abbey building.

Walnut Tree Cottage (so called from the tree in the back garden) probably dates from the 1860s and was occupied by farmworkers until the 1960s. It has been furnished to represent a typical farm labourer's home of the late 1940s. Its 'story', which you will find inside, focuses on the fictional characters of Bill and Mary Chapman and their family in 1949.

Living Room

The Second World War ended in 1945, but in 1949 many items – food, clothing, furniture – were still strictly rationed. The dining table and chairs were bought new in 1947, but most of the furniture dates from before the war. The furnishings in this room reflect the 1940s taste for cream and brown, popular until the 1950s. The walls are stencilled to look like wallpaper – something the Chapmans would have aspired to have but could have scarcely afforded (though the walls were so damp it would not have stuck on anyway). The brick floor is only partly covered by rag rugs, and the wartime spirit of 'mend and make do to save buying new' is still evident in various homemade and hand-me-down items. Notice the upturned stool used as the baby's high chair, and a photograph of the original on the wall. A prized item was the radio (wireless) set. Unlike many parts of Cambridgeshire, Denny had been on mains electricity since the 1930s, though electrical gadgets were not yet widely used. Instead of a refrigerator and vacuum cleaner, you will find, in the cupboard under the stairs, a meat 'safe' and carpet sweeper.

Kitchen

The family would have gathered in this room, rather than in the living room. It was usually warm thanks to the coal-burning range. The example here is Victorian, but new ranges were still being installed in cottages and local authority housing as late as the 1950s. The deep glazed kitchen sink has only a cold tap (though many cottages still used a pump over an outside well), hot water being provided by the kettle on the range. The house has no bathroom, so the sink also served for washing and shaving, and the weekly bath was taken in a tin tub on the floor. The multi-purpose kitchen cupboard, forerunner of the modern fitted kitchen unit, was a popular innovation from the 1930s onwards, with its many shelves, drawers and slide-out enamelled or Formica-topped work surface. Outside is a privy with a bucket: in 1949 the cottage had neither main drains nor septic tank.

Wash Room

Like some cottage people, the fictional Chapmans would have 'taken in' washing to earn extra money, hence the large amount of washing equipment here. Washdays began with the fire being lit under the copper, to heat the water. Hot water was scooped in to the non-splash wash tub, in which clothes were agitated by means of the wooden 'dolly' or copper 'posser' to rub out the dirt. Alternatively, the 'Housewife's Darling Washer' pounded the clothes at the turn of a handle. Soap was grated from solid blocks, though by the 1940s readymade soap flakes, like the Silver Leaves brand, were available. The laundry process finished – perhaps two or three days later – with mangling large items (the mangle here was already antique by the 1940s) and ironing with a range of irons heated on the range.

Bedrooms

Walnut Tree Cottage was built as a typical 'two up, two down' house, though another room downstairs (beyond the living room) served as a bedroom for some of the later occupants with large families. The bedrooms, probably always quite sparsely furnished, were very cold and damp in winter. Bed warmers, of the brown pottery or rubber hot water bottle type, were a necessity. The smaller, child's, bedroom has the luxury of a fireplace, though fires here were lit only in cases of exceptional need, such as sickness. The electric fire provided a little warmth in the parents' bedroom, though its bare element, fabric-covered flex and round-pinned plug would all be considered potentially dangerous today. As the cottage had no bathroom and only an outside toilet, the china chamber pot provided en suite facilities of a sort. One much older item displayed here is the Victorian iron baby's cot. This was probably borrowed from the abbey farmhouse: it was quite common for such items to be loaned or passed from family to family as the need arose.

The kitchen, with brick floor and deep glazed sink

The main bedroom, which the parents shared with the baby. Notice the bare floorboards covered only with homemade rag rugs

MUSEUM SHED DISPLAYS

From the cottage, passing the refectory to your right, go across the grass to the sheds by the gate.

❖ BASKET AND ❖ HURDLE MAKING

The Cambridgeshire fens are ideal for growing moisture-loving plants such as willow trees. By pollarding (cutting back) the tops of older trees, long straight poles were grown for use as hurdles – lightweight temporary fences with a variety of uses around the farm. Osiers, the young shoots of the willow, grow well on the wettest land. With their bark peeled off (a job often done by women and children in the field), they are ready to be woven into baskets. In the days before plastic containers, baskets had a great many uses, and basket making was a long-established craft in some Cambridgeshire villages.

Historic photograph of hurdle making in Cambridgeshire

CAMBRIDGESHIRE COLLECTION: CAMBRIDGE CENTRAL LIBRARY

The sheds were formerly used as loose boxes for horses and other animals, and in the 1960s the two farm pigs were kept here. Today they house displays about life in the Cambridgeshire countryside. Despite the 'high tech' image of Cambridge industry, the county is still predominantly rural in character. Eighty per cent of the land is used for farming, and the farms are mostly small in size – four-fifths of them cover 250 acres (100 hectares) or less. Cambridgeshire farming is also surprisingly varied. Root crops such as carrots, potatoes, celery and sugar beet grow well on the peaty fen soils, while elsewhere there is a long history of market gardening, fruit farming and flower growing. The Denny Abbey farm was more of a 'fen edge' mixed farm, with pasture as well as arable land and, during the ownership of the Chivers family, some fruit growing too.

Fenman's Hut

This reconstruction gives an impression of life in the Cambridgeshire fens before drainage schemes enabled almost all of the land to be farmed. Fen people known as 'slodgers' made a living from catching the abundant wildlife of the area, such as eels (from which Ely takes its name) and duck. The hut gives a view into a typical fenland duck decoy: a method of catching wild duck by luring them down a long net tunnel until they were caught at the end. Notice the collection of typical fen tools around the hut walls: some to help with drainage, others for jobs such as digging turfs, which were dried and used as fuel. There are also traps for catching rats, mice, moles, rabbits and birds.

Farrier's Workshop

Almost every village needed a blacksmith in the days when iron tools, fittings and machines were made, or repaired, locally. Many blacksmiths made horseshoes as part of their work, but strictly speaking this was the job of the farrier, who, although using many of the same tools as a blacksmith, was a specialist in horses. A trip to the farrier could save on a costly visit from the vet. A horse's hoof grows about a quarter of an inch a month and requires regular trimming; it was the farrier who was responsible not only for shoeing the

The reconstructed fenman's hut, with its diorama view into the 'pipe' of a duck decoy

horse, but for maintaining the health of the horse's feet.

As well as the blacksmith and farrier, most large villages had other skilled craftsmen such as coopers and saddlers.

Below left, the anvil, forge and cooling tray in the farrier's workshop

Dairy

Until recently most people had pints of milk delivered daily direct to their doorstep, rather than buying it from a

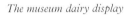

The museum dairy display

supermarket. In some places farm or country house dairies supplied the local demand for milk, butter and cheese. The museum dairy displays some typical equipment from churns to butter hands, all of which had to be kept scrupulously clean to avoid any risk of infection being transmitted.

Hand threshing of grain, or 'thrashing', on the barn floor. The man raises the hinged flail above his shoulder, then brings it down hard to thrash the corn and knock the grains off the stems and husks

Stone Barn

The stone barn is at the end of the shed displays.

In this barn, and elsewhere around the site, the Farmland Museum preserves and displays examples of the many tools and machines that were once so common on Cambridgeshire farms until a generation or so ago. The barn was built during the 17th century with stone from the abbey remains. This was a high-quality addition to the Denny farm buildings, with substantial walls and a complex roof structure. Notice how the oak roof timbers are pegged together: many are incised with Roman numerals at the joints. Like the other barn (the former refectory) there are double doors on opposite sides of the central threshing floor. When opened they provided an airy and well-lit working area, on either side of which was ample dry space for storing grain crops.

The farm tools and equipment shown here range from the centuries-old ox-drawn plough found in the tower of

CAMBRIDGESHIRE COLLECTION: CAMBRIDGE CENTRAL LIBRARY

The fruit farming display in the stone barn

Bassingbourn church to tractors and barn machinery that were in use within living memory. Many items such as hand-held scythes and rakes, or horse-drawn ploughs and seed drills, were once common throughout Britain. Most displayed here were made locally: in Cambridgeshire by agricultural engineers such as Maynards of Whittlesford and Coles of Ely, or elsewhere in East Anglia, by major manufacturers such as Ransomes of Ipswich.

The nature of Cambridgeshire farming, especially in the fens, often called for specialised tools and machines. The heavy ridged roller, for example, was used to flatten strips across the field for planting out celery, a crop that thrives in the rich, peaty fen soil. Growing and harvesting roots and vegetables was – and to some extent still is – a labour-intensive process. This seasonal work was often done by women, or by gangs of workers recruited and organised by gang-masters, a traditional system of labour still widespread in the region. The horse-drawn potato spinner, however, was a real labour-saving device. It flipped the potatoes out of the ground so they could be hand-picked from the surface, thus saving much back-breaking digging. Today the whole operation of lifting, cleaning and sorting the potatoes is done by a single machine.

Fruit growing also required special equipment, such as the sprayer, the wheelbarrow and the apple-picking bag, with its soft sides designed to prevent bruising of the fruit. The large black cart, one of a number of vehicles on display, belonged to John Fossey, fruit grower, of Eversden. Like many of the machines here, it was pulled by a horse. In 1938 there were still 19,000 horses working on farms in the county, and tractors and horses were to be seen working side by side in many fields until well into the 1950s.

At the south end of the barn are smaller machines designed for jobs that were often done under cover or during the winter months in barns and farmyards. Typical items include the chaff cutter, cake breaker and maize kibbler, all used for preparing animal feeds, and the bright blue

seed dresser, which cleaned seeds ready for planting the following season. The major winter task was that of threshing the grain – literally thrashing it on the hard floor with a flail of two hinged poles, to knock the grains off the stems. It was a tedious and exhausting job, but it kept the labourers in work through the lean winter months. By the mid-19th century steam-powered threshing drums (and, later, combine harvesters) had put paid to this manual work, and the number of full-time farm employees began a long decline. This process of farm mechanisation continues with ever-larger machinery, as a glimpse of the modern farmyard adjacent to the museum will reveal.

A selection of typical farm machinery, including a blue-painted seed dresser, in the stone barn

Young Farmers Club booklets dating from the 1950s, from the Farmland Museum archive

Village Shop Display

Leave the stone barn and go round to the shed on your left.

This display recreates something of the atmosphere of a typical village shop of the early or mid-20th century. At this time shopping expeditions by train, bus or cart to larger towns were occasional treats. Most country people relied on their village shops or delivery vans to provide for their daily needs. This was not a 'self-service' shop, as supermarkets were once known. Goods were requested over the counter and fetched by assistants, who were often dressed in brown coats and aprons. Nor were items bar coded for automatic checking. Prices were listed and sometimes labelled on goods, but had to be written on a paper till-roll, or (in more up-to-date establishments) recorded on a cash register. Most people paid in cash – then pounds, shillings and pence – though better-off people often had accounts that they settled monthly. There were no credit cards until the 1970s at the earliest.

So what could be bought at the village shop? The answer is just about every essential for daily living: some shops even had separate counters for drapery, shoes and hats. Many food items – such as sugar, flour, butter, tea, and dried fruit – were sold loose, prepared (notice the coffee grinder and currant cleaner) and weighed out on the counter. Popular with children were the tall glass jars of loose sweets: gobstoppers, aniseed balls, mint imperials, humbugs and liquorice allsorts. The shopkeeper used different scales or measures according to the weight or bulk of the goods, wrapping items in brown paper bags, or greaseproof or sugar paper. There were no plastic carrier bags as people brought their own shopping baskets – locally made, of course.

However, from Victorian times more goods came pre-packed. On some brands the packaging has changed little over half a century or more. Here you will find Colman's powdered mustard, Tate & Lyle's golden syrup, and HP sauce. Other

The museum's village shop displays many typical products from the 1930s to the 1950s. Small items were displayed in glass cabinets, while larger ones were kept on open shelves behind the counter, or even hung from the ceiling

❖ THE WHEELWRIGHT ❖

Leave the shop and go round the shed to the wheelwright and carpenter's display at the back.

Before the coming of motor vehicles, most village people depended on horse-drawn vehicles for transport. This ensured a brisk trade in building and repairing all sorts of carts and carriages. Wheelwrighting was a specialised trade requiring particular skills and tools, such as those for shaping the spokes, hubs and felloes (the rim pieces). However, in many villages, the wheelwright combined this work with general carpentry and could turn his hand to making anything from window frames to wheelbarrows, or even coffins. In fact, many carpenters and wheelwrights doubled as village undertakers. The items displayed here came from a wheelwright's shop in Quy. They include woodworking patterns, tools and a lathe powered from a hand-turned wheel perched on a platform.

The well-used wheelwright's work bench and tools

brands will be more familiar to older visitors. These include Sunlight and Lifebuoy soaps, Senior Service and Players cigarettes, Be-Ro flour, Lyons cocoa, Nuttall's mintoes and Bronco toilet rolls (or Bromo for those who preferred the loose leaf variety).

The shop also sold many types of ironmongery and home equipment for which there is little demand today. Behind the counter, or hanging from the rafters, are possers and rubbing boards for washing, wicks and glass chimneys for lamps, sandwich tins, thimbles and sock darning 'mushrooms', spare rubber rings for Kilner jars and a variety of enamelware

from bread bins to dustpans and chamber pots. Plastic products are notable for their absence.

CAMBRIDGESHIRE COLLECTION: CAMBRIDGE CENTRAL LIBRARY

A Cambridgeshire village shop in the early to mid-20th century

HISTORY

ROMAN DENNY

The first inhabitants of Denny are unknown, but before the foundation of the abbey the site would have been an island of firm land – or rather an archipelago of small islets – rising out of a watery landscape of peat fens and marshes. Though the surrounding area was not always flooded, raised banks or causeways were needed to connect one section to another. Sometimes passage was possible only by boat. The Romans, however, built a more substantial road just to the west of the site, and it is along this route that most visitors still arrive today. The many finds of pottery on the site suggest that a Roman settlement of some sort existed here, perhaps south or west of the abbey buildings, from the 2nd until the late 4th centuries. It is not known how the site was used after the Romans left, though the Domesday Book survey mentions that it was owned by one Eddeva in 1066, and from 1086 by Alan Rufus, 'the Red', one of William the Conqueror's right-hand men.

THE BENEDICTINE FOUNDATION

The monastic history of the site began shortly before 1159. At that time, the Denny lands formed part of a farming estate or manor centred on Waterbeach. This was then the property of one Robert, chamberlain to Conan IV, Earl of Richmond and Duke of Brittany. Though he was a rich and powerful man, Robert determined to end his days as a monk, perhaps hoping that this would help to save his soul for eternity. He established a small community of monks, drawn from the large Benedictine abbey at Ely, on his lands at Denny. Their living

Aerial view of the abbey, showing the remains of earthworks in the surrounding fields

© CROWN COPYRIGHT: NATIONAL MONUMENTS RECORD

accommodation would have been timber-framed and temporary, but work on the church must have started immediately. As was the normal practice, the masons began at the east end. By 1159, a sufficient part of the church had been built for it to be consecrated by Bishop Nigel of Ely and dedicated to Saints James and Leonard. Reynold, one of the Ely monks, was installed as prior, or leader, of the new community. Robert himself had retired as a monk to Ely, where he died soon afterwards.

ARRIVAL OF THE TEMPLARS

The Benedictine priory (named after St Benedict, who founded the order in 529) at Denny probably never had more than a few monks. Though they received an income from lands in Cambridgeshire and Yorkshire given by Robert the founder, for some reason the priory was not a success. Perhaps it was just too close to the main house in Ely to operate independently. About 1170 the Denny monks returned to Ely. Negotiations began between the Bishop of Ely, the founder's successors and the Knights Templar. In due course, the land, buildings and estates were all transferred to the Templars. The details of the agreement are not known, but no

doubt there were benefits to both sides. It is possible that the monks of Ely were in debt to the Templars – who, at this time, were famous for their banking operations – and Denny Abbey may have been used to pay off a loan, perhaps towards the huge construction costs of Ely Cathedral. Whatever the reason, it was a unique arrangement: Denny was the only property ever transferred directly to the Templars from another religious order.

THE TEMPLAR PRECEPTORY

When the Templars acquired Denny after 1170, they were at the height of their power and wealth. The prestige of the order, which did not come under the control of the bishops, was heightened by the fact that its castles in the Holy Land defended the Christian community there from attack. Most Templar communities were small and headed by a preceptor, and therefore known as

Left, manuscript illustration of a Benedictine monk at prayer, as shown by the words Ave Maria – 'Hail Mary'

This upper clerestory window once lit the nave of the Benedictine and the Templar church. Though originally an external window, it became an internal feature when the building was later remodelled

The scallop-pattern nave capitals (below left) are typical of the original Benedictine church. When the Templars completed the church, they changed the design to a waterleaf pattern (below)

The main west doorway of the church, as completed by the Knights Templar. Though badly worn, its elaborate carved decoration indicates the high status of the building

An illustration from a medieval French manuscript showing the arrest of Knights Templar

preceptories. They were set up to manage estates, collect money and recruit new knights. But as an existing monastery, with accommodation for several monks and a church at least part built, Denny lent itself to a different purpose. From early on it seems to have functioned as a sort of retirement home or hospital for elderly Templars, and its preceptor was possibly skilled in medicine rather than warfare. We can only imagine how knights who had served in the Middle East must have felt on retiring to the swamps and freezing mists of Denny.

The Templar community at Denny was probably never large, and there were just eleven members when the house closed in 1308. As there was no need for a grand church, the Benedictines' work on the church was completed with a nave only two bays long, probably rather shorter than originally intended. The leaf-shaped capitals and intricately carved (but badly worn) west door are Templar work. So too was the building originally to the south-west of the church, which was possibly the home of the priest who served the community. The living quarters were to the north of the church, and were quite spartan. When the Sheriff of Cambridge and Huntingdon arrived to close the house and arrest the Templars on 10 January 1308, he took an inventory of their possessions. He found eleven beds and one chest in the dormitory, two trestle tables and two 'tables dormant' (tables with fixed legs) in the refectory, plus a well-equipped kitchen and bakehouse. Only the church contents, including three silver chalices, a silk altar cloth and various sets of vestments, were an obvious sign of wealth.

CHANGES OF OWNERSHIP

For a time Denny's future looked uncertain. The last Templar residents were imprisoned first in Cambridge Castle, and then in the Tower of London, before renouncing their vows after 1311. In common with other Templar properties, Denny was handed over initially to the Knights Hospitallers, a similar order. They, however, made no use of it, and in 1324 it was taken over formally by the Crown. In 1327 Edward III granted it to a young widow, Mary de Valence, Countess of Pembroke. It was she who, in due course, established the third and final religious community at Denny.

THE COUNTESS OF PEMBROKE

The Countess of Pembroke, who also founded Pembroke College in the University of Cambridge, perhaps intended merely to add the Denny estates to those of the small nunnery at nearby Waterbeach, with which she was already associated. But Waterbeach was proving a difficult location: the nunnery buildings were low-lying and inclined to flooding. In 1339 the countess gained permission to transfer the nuns from Waterbeach to Denny, though several were apparently very reluctant to move. These nuns were known variously as Franciscans, Minoresses, or Poor Clares, after their founder St Clare of Assisi. They formed an enclosed order, dedicated to a life of prayer. There were also more members of the order – at least twenty-five, sometimes forty or more – than of the Templars, and major alterations and new buildings were thus required. It was at this time that the east end of the old Benedictine church was taken down and, in its place, a much wider and longer church built for the nuns. The countess then adapted most of the remaining old church into a private residence for herself, blocking up old arches and inserting new walls, floors and windows. A new guest hall replaced the south aisle of the old church, and the Templars' domestic buildings, including a cloister and

The Countess of Pembroke, kneeling before St Clare, from an illuminated medieval manuscript

CAMBRIDGE UNIVERSITY LIBRARY

refectory, were gradually enlarged or rebuilt. By the time of the countess's death in 1377 – she was buried before the high altar in the nuns' church – the abbey buildings were on a far grander scale than ever before.

THE POOR CLARES

As in the other two Poor Clare houses in England (in London and at Bruisyard, Suffolk), many of the Denny nuns came from well-to-do families. The life of a nun may have given them a sense of responsibility and control over their lives, which most medieval women lacked. The history of the nunnery is nevertheless largely uneventful. The farms and estates were, in practice, managed by a large staff, from stewards to farm labourers and servants. There were often disputes over land to be settled, and agreements drawn up such as

14th-century floor tiles on the floor of the nuns' refectory

The bread oven on the ground floor of the abbey, added when the building was converted to a farmhouse

James Essex's sketch of 1773 shows the abbey before the roof level was lowered and the nuns' dormitory, on the right, demolished

one in 1430, which described the tenants' responsibility to 'freely ferry in their boats all the ministers, officers and stewards of the Lady [abbess]' – a reminder that the fen surroundings remained undrained.

THE SUPPRESSION OF THE MONASTERIES

In 1535 commissioners arrived at Denny to survey the abbey for Henry VIII. They reported finding 'half a dozen nuns who, with tears in their eyes, begged to be dismissed'. The abbess at this time was Elizabeth Throckmorton, a formidable lady. Though most small monasteries were closed in 1536, Dame Elizabeth and some twenty-five nuns managed to hold out for another three years. When finally forced to abandon Denny in 1539, she and two or three nuns retired to her family home at Coughton Court in Warwickshire, where they continued to live the life of

enclosed nuns until her death in 1547. Meanwhile, the abbey was stripped of its contents, and the buildings and lands sold to an Essex property speculator, Edward Elrington.

LATER OWNERS

It was probably Elrington who set about systematically dismantling the nuns' church and some of the other buildings, selling off their valuable stone. Denny was saved from total destruction by the fact that part of the old church had already been converted into a house. With further modifications, notably the insertion of the large brick chimney on the south gable wall, it was easily adapted to serve as a farmhouse. In 1544 Elrington apparently returned the Denny estate to the king in an exchange of lands. It remained with the Crown until 1628, when Charles I transferred it to the City of London to repay a debt. Among those who leased the farm, and lived in the house, were Thomas Hobson (1544–1631), the famous Cambridge carrier. His refusal to allow customers to choose which horse to hire gave rise to the saying 'Hobson's choice'. Hobson's daughter Anne married into the prosperous Knight family; her son John Knight left his mark – literally – by carving his name neatly on a pillar in the abbey.

By 1675 Denny was owned by the Bacons, a London merchant family,

East View of Denny Abbey, taken by Mr. Essex in June 1773, before it was lowered a altered soon after by order of Peter Stanley, Esqr.

though it is doubtful if they ever lived here. The buildings and lands were leased out to a succession of farmers, and the stone barn (now part of the museum) was added for their use. In 1730 Thomas Bacon commissioned an engraving (see page 14) of the old refectory – with its little lectern wing and thatched roof still intact – which also gives an intriguing glimpse of the house beyond. In 1855 ownership passed to a Mr Coxell. It was probably in his time that the cottage was built to house farm labourers, while other workers lived in the row of cottages by the main road. By 1883 Denny was farmed by William Dimock, whose family were the last resident owners, farming here until 1929. Pembroke College, Cambridge, then bought the property. It was the college that put the farmhouse in the care of the Ministry of Works in 1947, though tenants continued to live in it until the 1960s. In the late 1960s parts of the buildings were dismantled to reveal the different building phases, the result being what is seen today. Some later farmyard buildings were also demolished, along with the western extension to the church, which had been added after it became a farmhouse. English Heritage took over guardianship in 1984.

Mrs Dimock entertaining friends to tea on the lawn by the farmhouse, about 1914. The house was once noted for its attractive gardens

FARMING AT DENNY

The Farmland Museum, opened in 1997, complements the abbey's earlier monastic history by telling the story of Cambridgeshire farming and rural life through the ages. Once religious life at Denny ceased in 1539, farming became the main concern of the abbey's occupants. Denny was well placed to benefit from the gradual drainage of the fens that began in earnest during the 17th century; some of the banks and ditches visible

The hall and living room of the farmhouse, with the ground-floor arch of the medieval church still evident

Strawberry pickers in the fields. The number of pickers, and the waiting horse-drawn carts, suggest that this was a large-scale commercial operation

The farmhouse and the yard, on the north side of the house, in the 1950s. Some of the post-monastic buildings that were later taken down are also seen here

across the fields are evidence of this process. The abbey farm itself, though, was a mixed fen-edge farm growing a variety of crops as well as raising animals. The higher land of the 'island' is firmly based on gravel and clay, ensuring good grazing for livestock. The surrounding lower land benefits from rich peaty soil, making it ideal for arable farming.

Diaries of families at neighbouring farms, such as that kept by the Wyatt family from 1902 to 1924, show how little farming here changed year by year. The same jobs – thrashing and chaff cutting through the winter, drilling (sowing) crops in the spring – were done almost on the same day year by year, subject only to the weather. Mechanisation came slowly. Horses were still used at Denny until the 1950s, and the first combine harvester was bought only in the 1960s. The Chivers

family, who farmed Denny during the 1940s and 1950s, used the fen-edge soils for fruit growing. They had begun commercial jam production as early as 1873, and their factory at Histon also made jellies and even Christmas puddings. No doubt they also grew peas here to supply their pea-canning factory in Huntingdon. Crops grown by Mr Martin, the current farmer, include wheat, barley, oil seed rape and sugar beet. These are 'rotated' round the fields to maintain the fertility of the soil and minimise the risk of disease. This is a process that even the medieval peasants who laboured here for the monks and nuns would have understood, though they might not have recognised the rape and beet crops. They would probably marvel at the short stems, large seeds and dense growth of the barley and wheat, the results of modern scientific research and advanced technology. Farming continues on the site with a modern farmyard adjacent to the museum.